A story about
a LITTLE soul
Who made a
BIG decision

www.moptoppublishing.com

A Story about a Little soul Who made a Big decision
Copyright © 2017 by Areyan

ISBN: 978-0-9876264-2-4

No part of this publication may be reproduced, distributed, or transmitted in any form or by any means, including photocopying, recording, or other electronic or mechanical methods, without the prior written permission of the publisher.

This book is dedicated to
Hanna
Thank you for choosing me

About the author

Areyan grew up singing to sheep on her grandfather's farm and dancing from as early as she can remember in New Zealand.

For many years she continued to follow her dreams performing, on stage and television and travelling until she became a mother.

Then, she changed direction and found a new expression through writing after searching for a book about finding your purpose for her five-year-old. Areyan didn't see that book, so she sat down and wrote it.

She lives in Sydney, Australia, with her daughter and dog and teaches ethics in primary schools.

About Laura Clark
(Illustrator)

Laura Clark is a Sydney born and based artist with an insatiable passion for the arts.

She has a broad range of interests and skills with professional qualifications in jewellery, sculpture, animation and 3D art. Alongside this she pursues other interests such as cosplay, singing and writing.

At the core of all this though is her love for drawing, something she's done since she could hold a pencil. Drawing and illustration has been a compulsion more than a hobby for all of her life, but this book is her first foray into published work.

Although currently exploring pathways in the video game industry, Laura hopes that this will be the first of many illustrative projects she will have the pleasure of working on.

Once upon a no time
there were two souls

This is Tu Nopsi

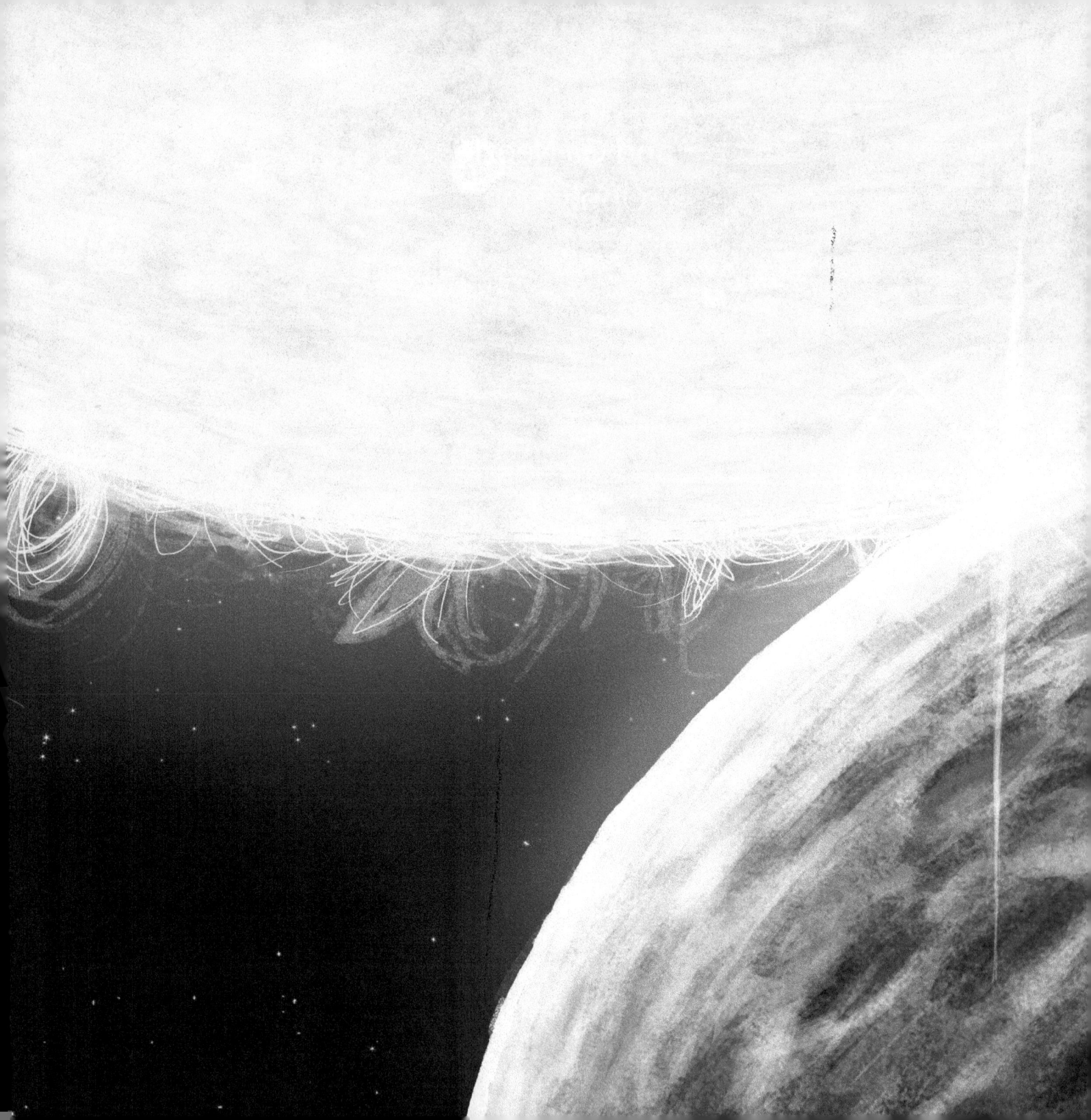

They live above
the woolly clouds

Above jet planes
that scream so loud
Imagine now
above all that...
and you'll take off
your gloves and hat

Our moon is up there
as big as the Sun
but one is MUCH bigger
can you guess which one?

SATURN

YOU ARE HERE → KUIPER BELT →

NEPTUNE

MARS
EARTH
MOON
MERCURY
VENUS

← ASTEROID BELT →

JUPITER

URANUS
PLUTO

MILKY WAY

BLACK HOLE & ORBITING STARS →

I assume
you have not seen
a zillion star galaxy
Not a popular destination
For human families

This is their home
called 'outer space'
but it's totally different
not like THIS place

They have no windows
white snow,
popcorn or walls
skateboards
play dough
TV or doors

No slippery slides
in which one can plummet
No ferris wheels
to make them both vomit

Now Ga Neezle and Tu Nopsi frolic
in this garden of heights
play with comets and meteoroids
and galaxy lights

They are wiser than the black crow
and extraordinarily happy
Royaller then royals married
in Westminster Abbey

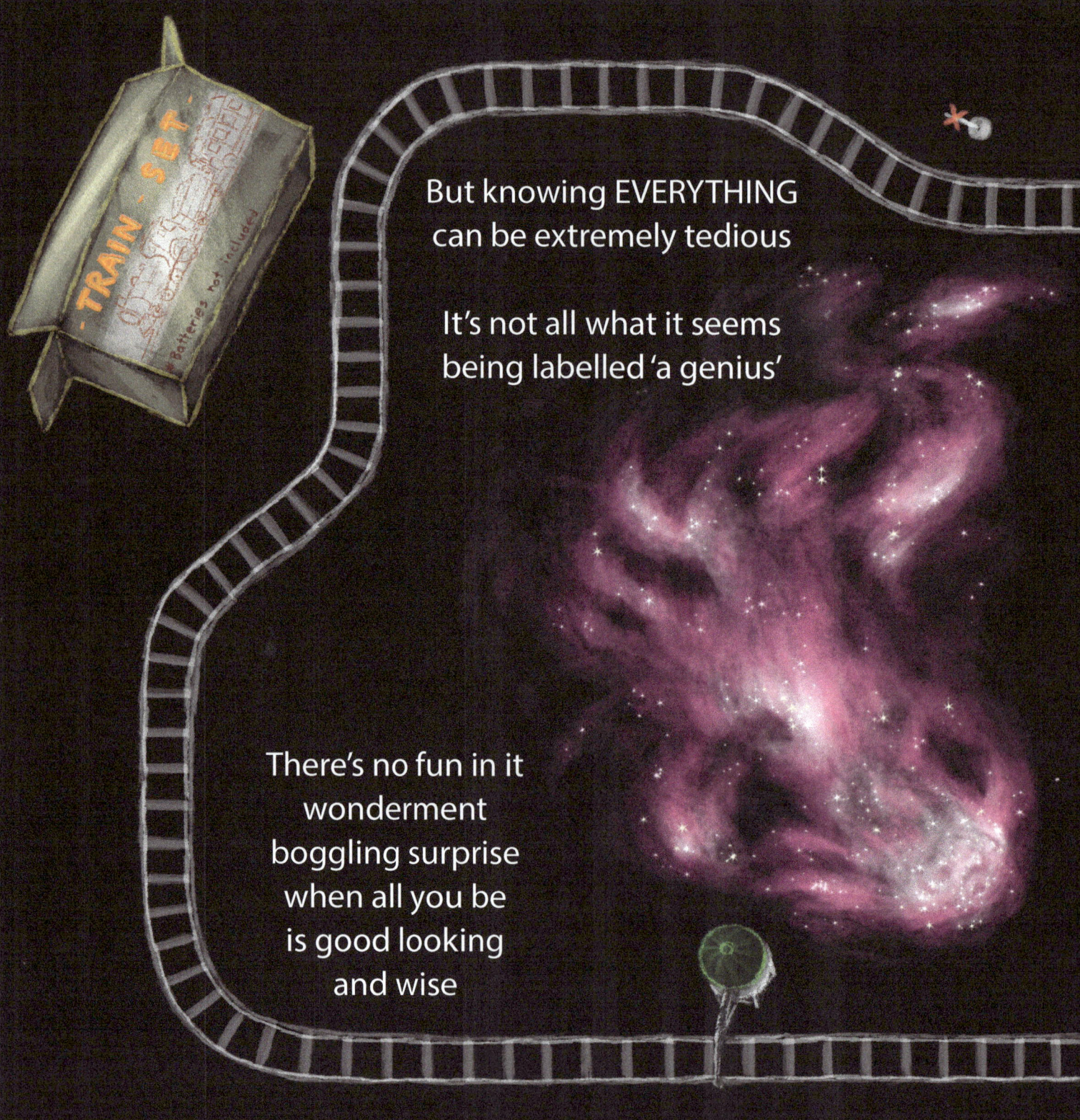

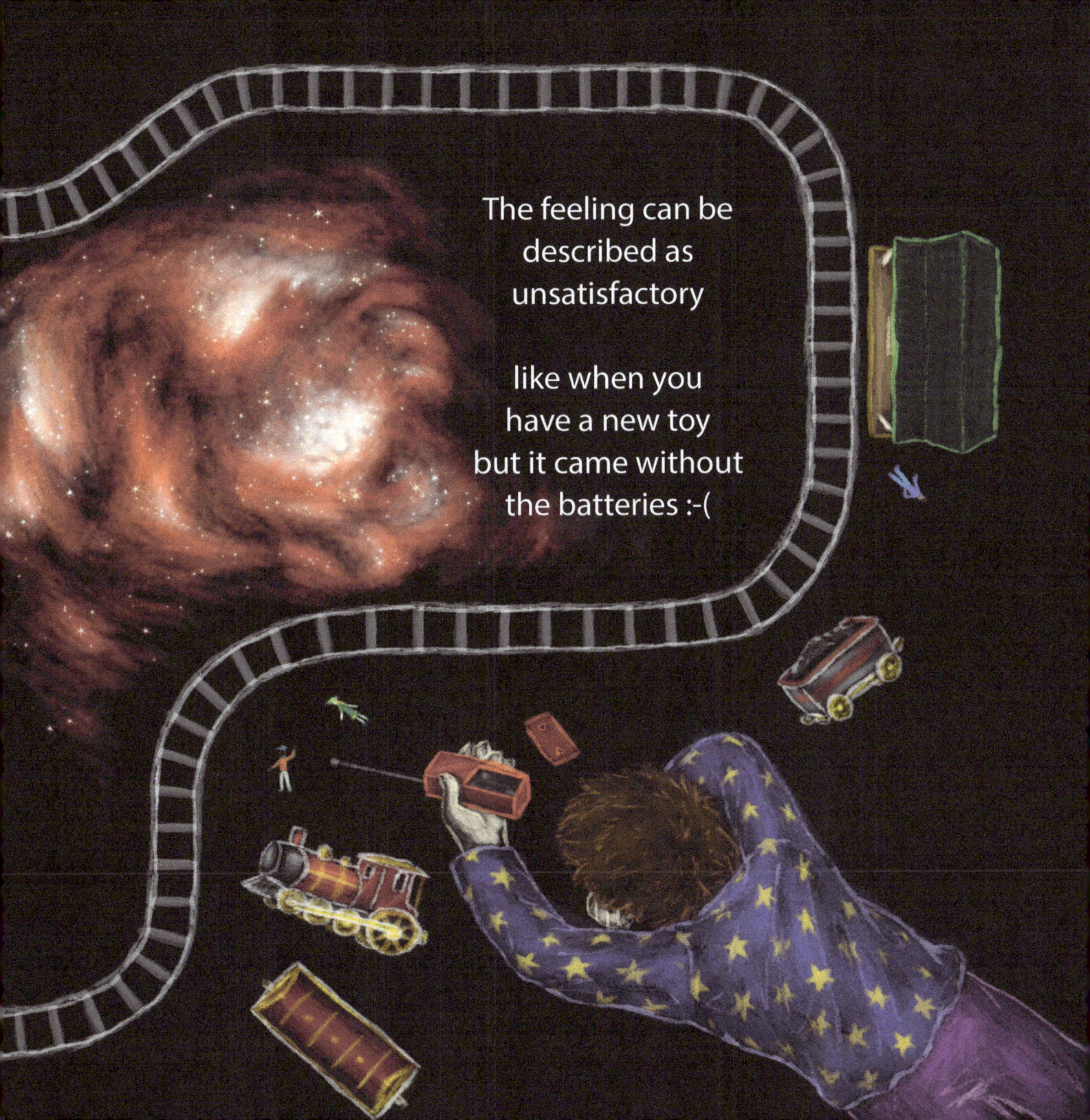

But they say nothing
they just watch
and observe
the bizarre things we
do
say
and eat
on planet earth

And what are feelings
Like the feeling of hot?

Is that like a temperature?
Or something you've got?

And what about snakes?...
is that a lizard with no legs?

I LOVE IT!
said Tu Nopsi
I want to live there

I want to
zoom down corridors
in a souped up
wheelchair

and so the

Soul Stars popped down
for their usual hovering

the basic snooping
and noseying
and general discovering

They found a
peculiar object
apparently a cucumber

and smuggled it
home to show….

Now Jordy is the largest
most spectacular colours of bellissmo

He comes in imperial purple
violet
blends of red
and indigo

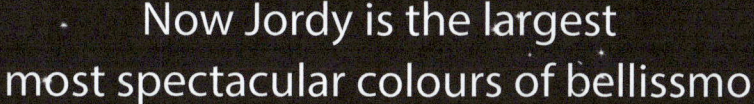

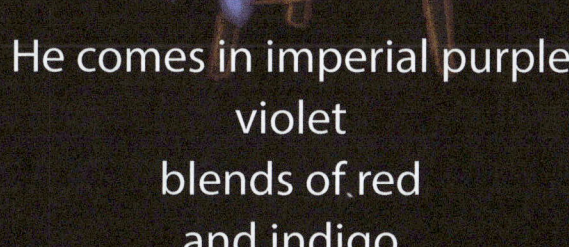

Tu Nopsi could not wait
to show Jordy the cucumber

The small greeny thing was a
welcomed newcomer

For Jordy knew
where it grew
and how to cook it
Cordon bleu
(that means fancy)

Jordy mumbled and bumbled the
most odd squeaky sounds

Jordy gets super enthusiastic
When discoveries are found

Waiting should not be a thing as time here does not exist

But that didn't stop Tu Nopsi that didn't stop her a bit

Just as she was thinking she could turn him into something thinnish

Jordy cleared his throat and announced with pride "I'm finished"!

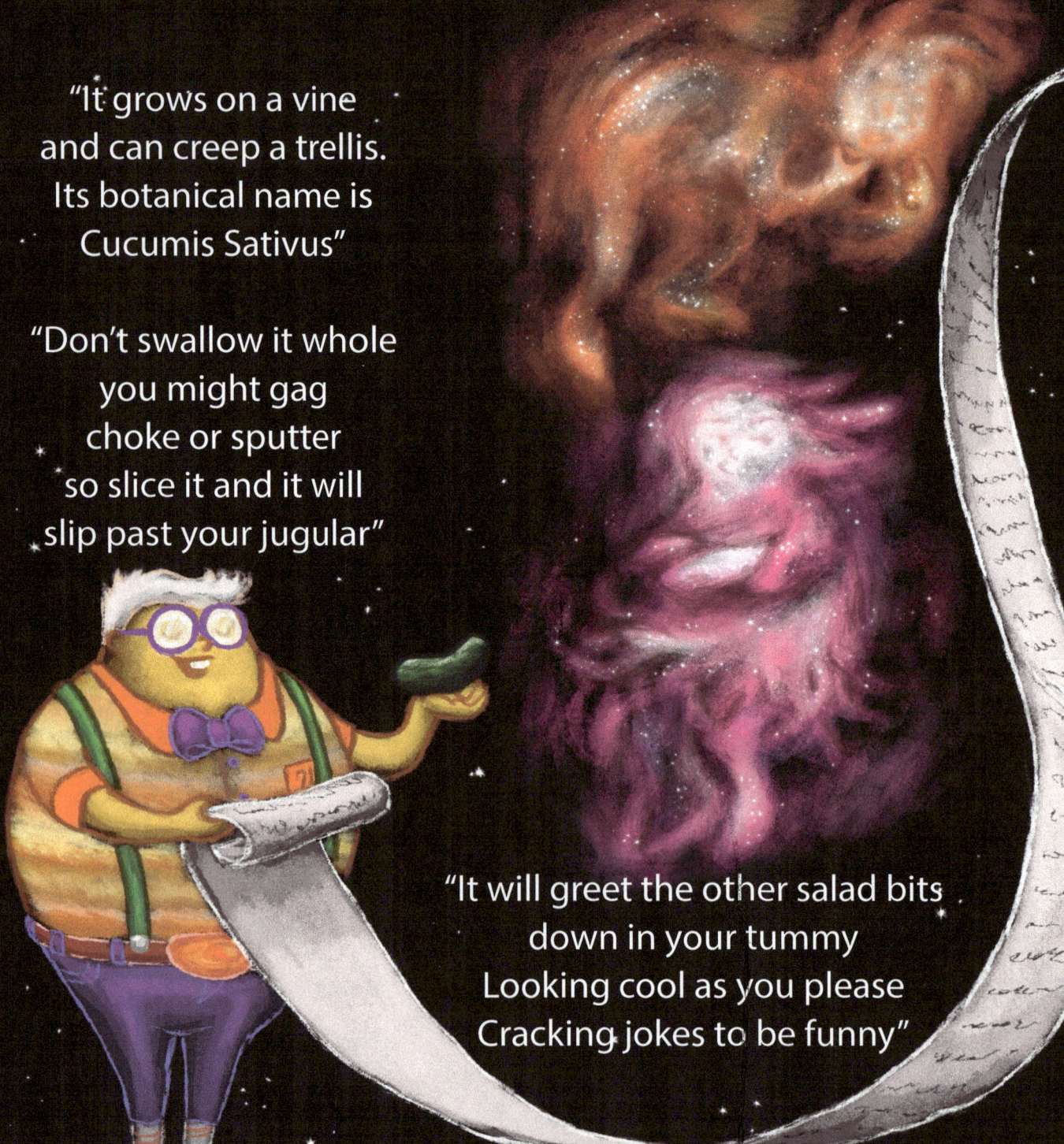

"It grows on a vine
and can creep a trellis.
Its botanical name is
Cucumis Sativus"

"Don't swallow it whole
you might gag
choke or sputter
so slice it and it will
slip past your jugular"

"It will greet the other salad bits
down in your tummy
Looking cool as you please
Cracking jokes to be funny"

Now Pluto is petite
her name is Janet
She is so small experts say
she's not really a planet

Although she be little
her power's are
tremendous

With Janet
things DO get
somewhat
horrendous!

she has been
known to take
asteroids to blend
into smoothies

Stroidjuice
makes her strong
But unfortunately
moody :-(

They told Janet their story
whether she cared
was irrelevant

In hindsight
veg shifting
was not very intelligent

Janet transformed the object
into something, somewhat bigger
something (she hoped)
to give the thing
A little bit of vigour

Now its features were challenged
it had eyes like a guppy
best known to earthlings
As DOG or ..

PUPPY!

It's teeth were large
and its ears were oddly hairier
the breed I believe is
Pit Bull Terrier

Ga Neezle froze

Tu Nopsi was not impressed

So Janet flicked her wrist
and...

Gave the dog a dress!

"That's better," she gleed
she thought her work impressive

But as usual
she was over-the-top
borderline excessive

The soul stars were now
really quite annoyed
the cucumber
was completely
and utterly destroyed

They stared at each other
couldn't believe it was ethical
this canine was once
a very small vegetable

"Janet!" they cried,
"what do we do with a pet?"

"a dog we can't pat
or feed
or play fetch?"

Janet thought... (for a tick)
shoulders shrugged... (or kind of)

Then suggested they 'be off' and ask the
GODDESS OF LOVE

The star gnomes were in trouble
in quite a dilemma

So they made a purple collar
with the name "Emma"

Venus shines beautifully being next to the Sun

You're *guaranteed* to feel
Zippy
Zoofy
and
a little bit good crazy

Tu Nopsi introduced
their hairy friend
they told their story
they were at wits end

Abbey's face was listening
but her thoughts
were thinking differently
The atmosphere stirred up
ever so gently

The wind gathered speed and
swept them all…

Now Venus has hair past her ankles
(which is cool but very weird)
and the tips of her hair touched Emma
who then
disappeared

Either Abbey didn't notice
maybe she didn't care
it was the soul stars who noticed

and here is what they said...

The moon came out
even the sun looked worried
Tu Nopsi had to find Emma
and to find her in a hurry

It was time to make decisions
would the souls follow Emma to Earth?

It would mean starting from the start again
which means
starting from birth

Tu Nopsi imagined a body
with a mouth
that made sounds

Two legs with knees
to do things like
sit down

Tu Nopsi could choose to be a girl or boy
maybe have a brother?
someone to annoy

" Um....Im not going…"
announced Ga Neezle
I've been there before
been all sorts of peoples

I like being here
It's so easy peasy
Being down there
gets kind of busy

People always telling you
What you should and should'nt do
At home
From your parents
And even at school

And when you grow up
They expect you to be
Anything you want
As long as they agree

So Tu Nopsi don't leave
It's not very clever
Stay here with me
And choose
freedom forever

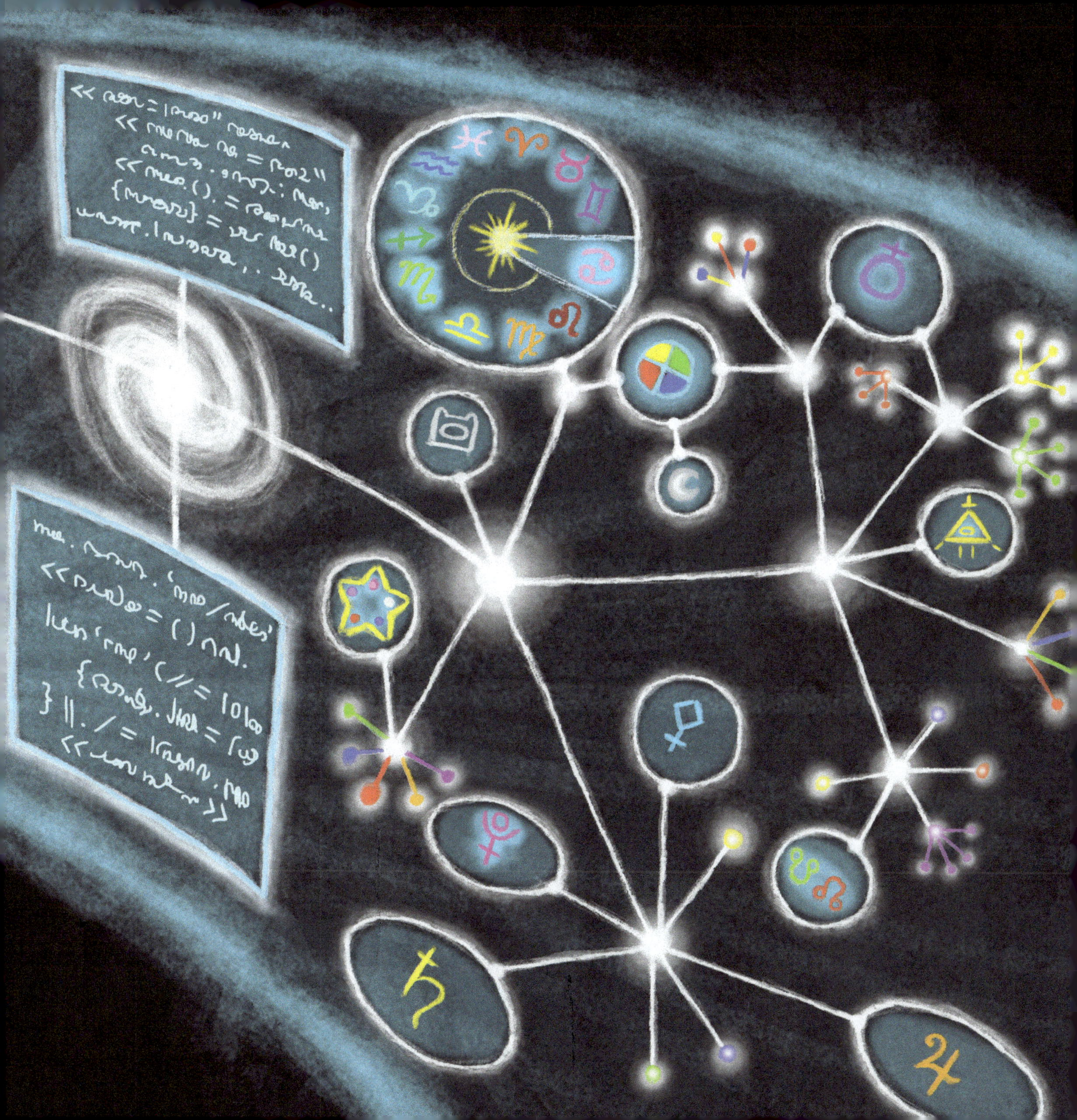

Tu Nopsi prepared for entrance
there was no paraphernalia
SHE set her course for Sydney
that's in Australia

Her memories were intact
but her soul felt shoddy
as she arrived to Earth
in a regular baby body

What a calamity!
the feeling of gravity
would Tu Nopsi completely
and utterly forget
that she is an immortal
space cadet?

Phara pher nalia (means with no special equipment)

"I vow" said Ga Neezle
spinning away in a comet
you'll NEVER be alone
its my most important promise

So
if you ever feel
teary and crappy
remember who you are
miss space cadetty

So next time you hold a baby
And they smile their gummy grin
remember they do more
then eat
sleep
and break wind

Take a closer look
swim in their eyes
close your own
and float inside

Now turn around
look back at you

YOU may be surprised
at the amazing view

You chose to come here
you're a perfect upgrade
everything you asked for
is in your DNA

And just because you're small
and start out
at age zero
in actual actualness
you're a supernova hero

Every detail about you
is part of the plan
your likes and your quirks
the small hairs on your hand

Before you came here
I don't know what you drew
and I'll probably guess
neither do you

But here you are
important and bright
so important the stars
come out every night

So too
does the moon
the Sun
the giver of light -
which is 400 times bigger
(but you knew that right?)

And in case you were wondering
whatever happened to Emma
she did come to Earth
with an urge
to be a singer

Whether you are here
There
Milan or Saigon
visit the link
We shall go to Amazon!
Stars of a different nature
Wait at your pleasure
Press all 5
★ ★ ★ ★ ★
Leave a rhyme
But no pressure

"we're Stars and we're Beautiful

Scan the QR code or visit below link:
https://www.amazon.com/dp/0987626426

www.ingramcontent.com/pod-product-compliance
Lightning Source LLC
Chambersburg PA
CBHW081940110426
42744CB00033B/1971